MYSTIC MICHIGAN
Part Seven
VII

By Mark Jager

Second Edition

MYSTIC MICHIGAN
PART SEVEN

By Mark Jager

Published by
ZOSMA PUBLISHING
PO Box 24
Hersey, Michigan 49639
zosmabooks@gmail.com

All rights reserved. No part of this book may be reproduced or transmitted in any form or by any means, electronic or mechanical, including photocopying, recording or by any information storage and retrieval system without written permission from the author, except for the inclusion of brief quotations in a review.

Copyright 2008, 2011 by Mark A. Jager
Second Edition Revised Volume Seven 2011

Cover Photo Michigan Dunes
By Deana Jager
Copyright 2010

ISBN13: 978-1507791257

Thou art worthy, O Lord,
to receive glory and honour and power:
for thou hast created all things,
and for thy pleasure they are and were created.
Revelations 4:11

Contents

Ancient War Mines	7
The Bottle House	9
Stone Chambers	11
Pre-Glacial Society	12
Turnip Rock	14
Eerie Pere Cheney	15
The Legend of Silver Mountain	17
Magnetic Abnormality	19
The Michigan Wizard of Oz Connection	20
Ancient Explosion	22
King Solomon's Mines?	24
Michigan's Brigadoon	26
Huge Statues	28
Echo Canyons	29
Wilderness Column of Water	31
Michigan's New Stonehenge	32
Amazing Dunes	33
Arrowhead Finds	35
The Orbs of Nunica Cemetery	37
Ancient Library of Rock	38
A Very Large Piece of Copper	39
Phenomenal Painting	40
Michigan's Lost Peninsula	42
Michigan's Continental Divide	44
The Mystic Rainbow	45
The River That Flows Both Ways	47

Ancient War Mine

Fred Rydholm, has written a new book entitled, "Michigan Copper The Untold Story" in which many interesting historical facts are covered. Perhaps one of the most interesting topics is that of ancient armies and their possible connection to historical Michigan.

Only about one percent of the copper mined from the Upper Peninsula of Michigan is accounted for. If this is the fact, where did it all go?

In his book, Rydholm theorizes where all the copper may have gone. Brass is made from copper; constituting two parts copper and one part zinc. Ancient armies required tons of it to forge nearly everything they used in battle. There were armies consisting of 200,000 to 300,000 soldiers, and each wore an average of 48 pounds of bronze. They used brass to forge helmets, shields and spears. Ancient navies lined the bottoms of their ships with bronze and some had ramrods aboard their war vessels made of bronze that weighed up to one-half a ton.

Other ancient empires may have used Michigan copper as well. Rydholm believes that the Minonens Empire was the first to mine copper from Michigan. They were from the Island of Crete during the reign of King Minus. After a volcano destroyed their civilization, the Phoenicians came in and took over. During this period, the Phoenicians may also have mined the copper for King Solomon. Other ancient cultures such as the Celts and Norsemen also mined copper in Michigan later.

There are several theories that Michigan copper was used for everything; from forging tools to build the Great Pyramid, to creating King Solomon's temple, to weapons for massive armies. On Rhoads Island, in the eastern Mediterranean, there once was a giant statue in the harbor called Colossus that was constructed entirely out of brass. It is possible that the materials used to create this monumental structure were mined in Michigan.

The Bottle House

Did you know that there is a house in Michigan made out of pop bottles? Glistening in the sun on Wuoski Avenue in Kaleva, Michigan stands a wonder of art. In the early 1940's, a man named John Makinen owned a pop bottle company. He must have been industrious, frugal and not least of all, artistic. He constructed his "Happy Home", as is inscribed on the front of the home, out of 60,000 glass pop bottles. Mr. Makinen's home is so fascinating that it has been mentioned in both the Historic Register and in Ripley's Believe-it-or-Not

This unique home was built upon a concrete foundation and has a traditional roof. Although the majority of the exterior walls are constructed out of bottles there is also some traditional siding and of course windows. The bottoms of the bottles face out and the different colors of each bottle create a beautiful design. The "Kaleva Bottle House" is not only unique, but is also an inspiration that testifies to the workmanship of the 1940's. John Makinen took the time and effort to build something extraordinary that still stands nearly 80 years later. Makinen died in 1941, and he is still inspiring people.

This humble and distinctive home is a unique asset to the little community of Kaleva. In 1980, the home was purchased by the local historic society. It now serves as a lumbering museum open on weekends from 12-4 PM April through December. However, you can take a drive by and view the creatively structured home any time of year

Stone Chambers

Deep within the wild forests of Michigan, a number of people have happened upon peculiar, ancient stone chambers. Several have been discovered throughout Michigan's Upper Peninsula. One was cloaked by the forest upon Huron Mountain. Another was discovered near the Escanaba River, in Ontonagon. Others are located near Munising and the Rock River. One was even found near Rockford, in Michigan's Lower Peninsula.

These unusual stone structures are three or four feet high, and four or five feet wide with a beam going across the top of the entryway. Michigan historian, Fred Rydholm, theorizes the chambers are of a Celtic origin and were used for religious purposes.

There are numerous similar structures on the eastern coast of the United States that Rydholm believes could be associated to the ones here in Michigan.

Pre-glacial Society

There are many different theories, from both private and public research, concerning some of the different relics that are found in Michigan. These relics have prompted growing interest in recent decades, about what different cultures have lived here throughout history.

There is the traditional belief that only various tribes of Indians have dwelt here. Others say that there was a Caucasian race that pre-dated the Indians. Some say that refugees from the lost continent of Atlantis fled here. I personally believe that a technologically advanced people lived here whose civilization was destroyed. I believe a lot of the traces of this highly advanced society have vanished.

In a conversation I had with Michigan Historian, Fred Rydholm, I was told of a new theory; that of a pre-glacial society. Rydholm informed me of a man from Traverse City who believes that a group of people lived here before the glaciers came through.

"There is a man who has been going along the shoreline of Lake Michigan, Huron, and Superior finding strange shaped rocks that he believes are from some ancient society," Rydholm says. "He has sent me photographs of various rocks he has found. He claims that there are rocks arranged in circles underneath the water in various places within the Great Lakes."

Rydholm says he has no way to prove or disprove what the man says he has discovered. "I try not to discourage people, he may be on to something." Rydholm has a good point. If someone is encouraged to explore this is positive. Although many theories eventually are dismissed, some of them actually end up being a true interesting discovery. Adventure adds to ones quality of life.

Turnip Rock

Talk about being put on a on a pedestal! There is a tiny, yet majestic island located in Port Austin, in Huron County, Michigan that is such a special place that it actually sets on a natural stone pedestal. Set atop a mammoth podium, rising up out of the sparkling blue waters of Lake Huron, is the bowl-shaped island of Turnip Rock. It is an ecological monument in the midst of a great inland sea.

What shaped this intriguing formation? The age-old natural podium harkens to some colossal geological event that occurred at some remote time in Michigan's past.

One cannot help but wonder how this fantastic natural structure was perceived by the people and cultures of Michigan's past. What did the Indians think of this preeminent piece of land? What lore may have been created around this grand structure by ancient mariners that sailed past this nautical monument? It is as though the massive stronghold rises up out of the vibrant waters like a watchtower for some mystic guardian of the sea.

One can imagine sitting atop this exclusive platform having a sunset campfire overlooking the beautiful waters of Lake Huron. However, for the realist, boat tours are available.

Eerie Pere Cheney

Over the past several years I have received a number of reports of a ghost town near Grayling, Michigan named Pere Cheney. This forgotten community, presumed to be the first settlement *(est. 1869-70)* of Crawford County, was located about seven miles southeast of Grayling. With a population of 60, the small town had a post office, hotel, sawmill, wagon shop, a blacksmith and a grocery store.

Today, when people visit the area they claim that strange phenomena take place. Some declare they have photographed and videotaped blue orbs. People even assert to see the orbs with the naked eye. Visitors to the location have also had unusual problems with electrical equipment, radios and other devices. Others report that the wind suddenly stops and starts. Some people experience strange changes in the temperature.

Several allege that a sound phenomenon takes place at the cemetery in Pere Cheney. When one stands outside of the cemetery gates, a variety of sounds can be heard. However, once you enter through the gates and into the cemetery, it is *dead* silent. Some go as far as to say that they have heard voices and found sandy handprints on their vehicles upon leaving.

There are a number of ominous rumors concerning Pere Cheney, however you can draw your own conclusions with an intrepid visit to the location yourself!

The Legend of Silver Mountain

Through the mists of time, a Michigan legend has survived. Strange tales come down through generations concerning Silver Mountain, near Baraga, in Michigan's Upper Peninsula.

Silver Mountain stands towering, patiently minding the crystal waters of the Sturgeon River gorge like a solemn sage. Those with the fortitude to make the climb up this majestic tribute are richly satisfied with a panorama and serenity that is vast. The stunning wilderness that encompasses the mountain continues infinitely in all directions.

A trek through this wild terrain provokes primitive adventure. Hikers, that retrace their footsteps, have discovered both cougar and wolf tracks embedded in their own footprints a mere five minuets after they have passed through.

There are testimonies of significant amounts of silver to be discovered on *Silver* Mountain; hence the name. In the 1800's silver was mined from a cave located on the mountain. Bizarre superstitions have evolved from strange events that have taken place there.

A mystery began, that incited unease and Native Americans lore, when a large boulder somehow blocked the entrance to the cave. While the mine was still in operation, the Native Americans claim to have seen a glowing light permeate from within the cave. They refused to go near Silver Mountain, believing that evil spirits inhabited the cave. The ancient legend states that the gods placed the boulder at the entrance to keep people out. The boulder maintains, obstructing the entrance to the cave and concealing any secrets the primitive mine may hold.

Among Michigan's many fantastic natural resources; including lakes, rivers and streams; hiking, biking and nature trails; Silver Mountain is set apart by its rustic and wild beauty. Adventure, tranquility and even a little mystery are attainable upon the majestic peaks and valleys of Silver Mountain in Michigan's Upper Peninsula.

Magnetic Abnormality

According to Dave McConnell of Rockford, there are certain areas in Michigan where anomalies take place in the earth's magnetic field.

McConnell spoke of a couple of places in Michigan where magnetic abnormalities take place. "I know a man who works for a cable company who was setting up a satellite near a trailer park south of White Cloud. He got out his compass to set it up, and the compass began spinning wildly out of control. He returned to the site again later and the compass did the exact same thing. Both times his compass broke; it would not point to true north."

McConnell claims there is a similar place on top of a hill near Rodney. It is said that odd things happen in the area surrounding 138th Street. "There are people in the area who claim that they've seen balls of light come right into their barn. There were U.F.O. sightings for two weeks straight in 1993 at the location," he said.

The Michigan *Wizard of Oz* Connection

Michigan is the home of many magical places. It is no surprise that it has been called a "Wonderland'. The mystery and charm of this state is incredible. Few places in the world contain as many serene, beautiful and odd places as Michigan.

Is it any wonder that the inspiration for the movie *The Wizard of Oz* came largely from Michigan? That's right! L. Frank Baum, the author of the *Wizard of Oz* based many of the features of his book (which later became the movie) on the places he enjoyed at his cottage in Macatawa Park near Holland, Michigan.

L Frank Baum spent many of his summers in the early 1900's at the cottage According to a newspaper article in the Holland Sentinel from 1989, Munchkin land was pattered after, and inspired by the cottages of Castle Park (Macatawa Park). There is also a beautiful castle that was the inspiration for the *emerald castle*. The roads in the quaint neighborhood were at one time made of yellow bricks, subsequently, the idea for the world famous *yellow brick road*. These days, Macatawa Park holds *Wizard of Oz* festivals.

The author drew comfort and inspiration from the magic of Michigan. It is fascinating to know the idea for the classic story was derived from a small community in Michigan.

Michigan has still further connections with this unique childhood story. Ray Bolger, the actor who played the scarecrow, found respite a little further north in Michigan. He owned a cabin retreat near Lake Mitchell in Cadillac.

The next time you watch "The Wizard of Oz", just remember it was inspired, in part, by a place in Michigan. Now, click your heels together three times and say, "There's no place like Michigan"!

Ancient Explosion

A Michigan man believes he has made a discovery that could rewrite history. Dr. William Topping, a retired University Professor of Nuclear Physics was doing experiments at a site near Grand Blanc, Michigan when he ran across something very extraordinary. He originally thought he had located a World War 2 bomb-testing site. What he actually found ends up being something very different.

Topping consulted with Richard B. Firestone of Lawrence Berkely National Library in California concerning his findings. They conducted experiments at the National Superconducting Cyclotron Laboratory, and Phoenix Memorial Laboratory at the University of Michigan. Their research seems to indicate that a great destruction took place in Michigan thousands of years ago.

What kind of destruction? Their investigations indicate that the entire Great Lakes region was subjected to an ancient nuclear catastrophe, primarily centered in Michigan. The area showed evidence of blast patterns in the rocks that are only produced by a nuclear explosion. The plutonium and uranium levels found in the soil confirmed the possibility of a nuclear explosion in Michigan's earliest history. Topping also found what appear to be ancient computer chips at the impact site near Grand Blanc. Could this be the result of an ancient meteor impact or a deliberate nuclear explosion created by a civilization that was more advanced than what most think?

Records of the scientific research on the explosion can be found in a book entitled "The Cycle of Cosmic Catastrophes" by Richard B. Firestone. There is also the report; "Terrestrial Evidence of a Nuclear catastrophe in Paleo-Indian Times", that can be viewed on the internet.

King Solomon's Mines?

Historic records indicate that sixteenth century Jesuit priests discovered thousands of worked copper mines on Isle Royale, in Michigan's Upper Peninsula. Neither the Jesuits nor the Indians of the time knew who had removed 500,000 tons of copper from these mines.

To add to the mystery, the tons of copper have gone missing. Only one percent of that particular copper has ever been found in the United States. If it is not in the US, then where did it all go?

Author, Henriette Mertz found that carbon 14 dating of the organic matter, taken from the mineshafts at Isle Royale, indicate the copper was mined around the time that King Solomon's temple was built. Among other researchers, Walter Baucum, also believes that the copper was mined during the "golden age" of Israel. At that time, Israel and Phoenician navies sailed around the world collecting gold, silver, and copper for King David and King Solomon. The copper was used to make bronze for use in constructing the massive temple. It is very possible that the mines on Isle Royale were mined by King Solomon's navies. It is inspiring to consider that resources from Michigan may have played a significant roll in the construction of one of history's most magnificent structures.

Michigan's Brigadoon

There was once a beautiful and picturesque village in Michigan surrounded by water. The little village was called Muskegon Forks. Although unseen, it actually still exists near modern Croton, Michigan.

It is said that those who traveled through Muskegon Forks long ago, described it as being a pretty town with beautiful homes surrounded by white picket fences. The area was pleasant and set at the forks of both the little and big Muskegon Rivers.

However, this town has disappeared. Where is it? It lies at the bottom of the lake in Croton. The village vanished forever on August 9, 1907 when the waters from a new dam covered the town. Some of the residence had lived there for many years. The landscape they had called home quickly became only a memory after a dam was constructed.

In the late 1800's, when the logging era began to fade, many of the buildings in the once quaint town fell into disrepair. Later, in 1899, a fire destroyed 18 buildings. At that time, a company stepped forward and proposed to build a dam with the support of the local people. The area was flooded and a new town sprung up. It was named Croton after the hometown of the postmaster, who had once lived in Croton, New York.

    Underneath the waters on the east side of the causeway in Croton, lie remains of Muskegon Forks. It is unknown how many buildings are still under water. Perhaps someday in the future, if the dam were to be removed, the historical remains of a once thriving town would reappear.

Huge Statues

Did you know that the largest statue of a Native American on the planet Earth is in Michigan?

That's right, there is a large fiberglass Indian in Ironwood that weighs around nine tons. It stands over 50 feet tall. The figure, named "Hiawatha" stands like an ancient guardian at the entrance to an old historic mine. The figure towers over top of nearby homes.

He is just one of many mammoth statues in Michigan. One of the largest crucifixes in the world can also be seen in Michigan at "The Cross in The Woods' near Indian River.

Several giant wooden chairs, crafted by a Michigan wood worker, are located in numerous places throughout Michigan. One of them can be seen in Gaylord in front of an area business named Twiggs and Blooms. On Highway 10, just east of Reed City, stands a huge knight.

You may see just about anything in Michigan. How about a giant golfer that stands in front of the Riverbend Driving Range in Chesterfield? In Dundee, at the Cabela's Sports Shop, there is a huge statue of a bear at the entrance of the store.

Echo Canyons

Very few people are aware of the fact that an incredible echo phenomenon exists in canyons hidden in Michigan's Upper Peninsula.

Greg Wright is a hunting guide who has been exploring the peninsula for years. He shed light as to where some of these canyons can be found. There are canyons near Baraga, Marquette, and one off the Maple Creek Canyon.

Miner's Canyon, off the Miner's River, is near Munising. When a person shouts into the canyon, their voice carries. When the echo comes back, it sounds as if someone is answering from three or four miles away. On a calm day, up to six to eight fantastic echoes can be produced as the sound waves bounce off the rocks. The last echo heard is one that hits a sheer rock wall around a corner. The rock wall is a cliff that drops about 600 feet straight down. When a persons' voice bounces back off the rock wall it sounds just like someone is yelling back. This echo has been explained as being hair rising. Wright describes hearing eagle cries, echoing through the canyon, as an unforgettable experience.

Fig. 1

Fig. 1 Looking out from the top of Echo Canyon.

Fig. 2 From the base of Echo Canyon.

Wilderness Column of Water

There are incredible water features that can be observed in the western Upper Peninsula. They are located in remote areas and do not receive a lot of publicity. Tourists cannot find them unless a guide or a local brings them there.

Greg Wright and his family have explored some of these secret areas. They have found a place near pictured rocks they like to visit. At the location, there is a sheer cliff with a small stream cascading over it. The stream drops straight down and forms a small column of water, like a pillar, that descends about 100 to 150 feet. Wright says he has seen this column of water vary between six feet and one and a half feet wide.

One of the incredible things about it is that the majority of people do not know about it. If a person were to go out there, they may quite possibly enjoy the location, for days, with no one else around.

"We have been fishing at the bottom of waterfalls that are somewhat secretive. We pull in one fish after another for hours. We've never even seen anybody else there, even in the middle of the summer", says Greg.

Michigan's New Stonehenge

There are many unusual monuments in Michigan. Some of them are ancient while others are modern. In Mystic Michigan Part One I mentioned that in the early 1990's a rock formation was found on Beaver Island that some researchers believe was an ancient calendar similar to Stonehenge. In other editions, various earthworks in Michigan were written about. However, did you know that there is a Stonehenge in Michigan made out of foam?

Fred and Pam Levin of Nunica, Michigan were inspired to duplicate the monumental Stonehenge of England. It took them about a month and a half to construct a small-scale version of the prehistoric site in their own front yard. They sculpted Styrofoam then covered it with stucco and paint to create the faux-stones that stand about thirteen feet tall. Although it is about half the diameter of the original, it is correctly proportioned to their yard.

Kindly respect the Levin's private property and view their Stonehenge sculpture from Leonard Road, south of Nunica.

Amazing Dunes

It is not common knowledge that the second highest sand dune in the world is in Michigan. Grand Sables Dunes, near Grand Marai, are second only in height to the dunes in the Gobi Desert.

Not too many people realize how amazing Grand Sable Dunes are. Huge sand storms take place there that rival the sand storms in any major desert.

There are all kinds of amazing sights at the dunes. If you have ever wanted to see a river coming out of the side of a sand dune, Grand Sables is the place to see it. Along a thirteen-mile stretch there are rivers, ranging from two to ten feet wide, gushing out of the dunes. The streams come out of nowhere. The area rivals other awesome places of its kind anywhere on the planet.

These remarkable dunes are distinctively wild Michigan. Mountain Lions, wolves, bears and coyotes are common. These majestic predator animals are close at all times in the region. Hunters who visit the area report the sensation of being watched.

A visit to the Grand Sable Dunes and Grand Sable Lake will provide adventure and a glimpse of pristine Michigan.

Arrowhead Finds

Doug Mills of Bellaire never really thought about Native Americans and their history until about 2001. He thumbed his nose at nature, and really did not care about local history.

Until one day when he decided to go for a swim in Torch Lake. After going for a dip he sat on the shore and watched the boats go by. He tried to get a more comfortable seat on the shore, and positioned his hands behind him for balance.

He noticed a strange rock with a glassy brown texture and recognized that it was no ordinary rock. He studied it and identified that it had been hit with a primitive tool repeatedly. Prompted by his curiosity he went to the library and began studying about the tribes and people who had once inhabited Michigan. He continued to read and pay closer attention to rocks he found along the shore.

Before long, he understood the stone-people/ Indians who had lived here and the reasons why they hunted, fished, farmed and built a life from the forests. As time has gone by, he has located more broken points, chipped pieces, and unusual shapes near the waters edge. He has concluded that the Native American culture of this area was much more intuitive, intelligent, and inventive than what he once thought.

    Mills says the shorelines are filled with broken tails, half made pre-forms and unusual artifacts. Mills believes that we must not be blind to what is right underneath our feet when we walk along a stone filled shoreline in Michigan. He hopes that more people will pay closer attention to our local Native American heritage. Those who wish to take the time to look may discover that there are some interesting Indian artifacts to be found along the shores of many Michigan lakes.

The Orbs of Nunica Cemetery

A growing number of people have observed a strange lighting phenomenon at the Nunica cemetery.

Peculiar orbs of light have been seen and photographed. Newspaper articles and internet reports have fueled the popularity of this bizarre spectacle.

The Holland Sentinel did an article on the bizarre episodes occurring in the cemetery on October 22, 2003. They interviewed people who said they had seen apparitions of various kinds and strange mists. Self-proclaimed "paranormal investigators" conducted further research of the location with various electrical devices.

There has also been a lot of speculation concerning the strange events. What people are actually experiencing is a matter of opinion and investigation. Perhaps the lighting phenomenons have something to do with the power lines that run behind the cemetery. Another thing to consider is that if a digital camera photographs dust particles, the flash of the camera will cause the dust particles to appear as an orb of light on the photograph.

Perhaps a late night trip to the Nunica Cemetery could help you draw your own conclusions.

Ancient Library of Rock

According to geologists, Michigan was once much closer to the equator. Certain areas were covered with shining prehistoric seas. Grand Rapids was covered with a shallow marine sea. The sea deposited shale, gypsum, and limestone.

The body of water was restricted to a basin that had limited circulation. After a large amount of evaporation, the water eventually disappeared.

Deep down underneath Grand Rapids is an ancient geological record preserved in stone. There a geologist can observe various layers of rock that all tell an ages old story to the trained geological eye. This library of information is written in rock by divine fingers. There are different types of minerals and even plant fossils thousands of years old.

They can all be seen in the gypsum mine eighty feet beneath Grand Rapids. There are nearly six miles of tunnels in the underground now owned by Michigan Natural Storage. With planning and permission, you can enter this underground world, and read the geological hieroglyphics written in stone. This information was hidden for centuries, but is opened in the modern day for your enjoyment.

A Very Large Piece of Copper

A huge piece of copper was discovered south of Calumet in 1997. The hunk of copper is estimated to weigh from 40 to 50 tons. That is around 100,000 pounds!

There has been a lot of interest in the copper nugget. Most of the intrigue is coming from the Ancient American Artifact Preservation Foundation. They are trying to purchase the gigantic piece of copper to use as a centerpiece for a museum that will exhibit pre-Columbian artifacts.

The piece of copper was originally for sale for one million dollars. However, the AAAPF negotiated a more reasonable price.

One may wonder how a 40 to 50 ton piece of copper is going to be moved to a museum. The AAAPF has a solution. They are going to construct the museum around it!

Phenomenal Painting

A very interesting painting hangs on the wall of Bear Lake Christian Church near Grayling. The story behind the painting is very intriguing as well. David Harrington of White Cloud first brought this painting to my attention. A few years later, David Rosenberg of the Grayling area filled in the details.

This is how the story behind the painting goes. Donna Critchfield was on her way back from Mayo clinic. According to reports, she was miraculously healed of cancer. She says she was given a vision of a painting she was to paint of Christ. The painting was of Jesus Christ standing in a doorway on top of a porch that has several steps going up onto it. In the doorway that he is standing in there are doors.

One evening there was a woman working at the building where the picture hangs. She says that as she was working, she noticed the doors on the picture moving. After awhile more people started noticing the picture move.

David Rosenberg spoke of the painting. "When you stand on the right side of the room where the painting hangs, the doors on your side look like they are open wider than the doors on the other side. The same thing is true when you stand on the other side of the room. You can watch the doors close and open."

Rosenberg also mentioned that if you are standing on the right side of the painting, it looks as if a set of stairs come straight at you. Another set of stairs seems to go off at an angle. If you go to the other side of the room, the same thing happens. What makes this strange in Rosenberg's opinion is that the woman who painted the picture, Donna Critchfield, did not design the painting like this on purpose. She did not even know that the painting did this until someone else pointed it out to her later.

It is true that there are many non-religious pictures that do this type of thing. However, most of those paintings are made like that on purpose. The purpose of writing this story is not to venerate a painting. It is just interesting, and brings into your thoughts a number of unique possibilities.

Michigan's Lost Peninsula

"The Lost Peninsula" is a part of Michigan that is separated from the rest of the state. You have to drive through the state of Ohio in order to get there. Traveling south in Ohio, on I-75 towards Toledo, take exit 2 and merge onto Summit St.; go 3 miles then turn left onto 131st st.; go ½ mile then turn left on to Edgewater Dr. where you will soon cross from Ohio into Michigan's Lost Peninsula.

The Lost Peninsula came to be after the "Toledo War" (1835-1836, also known as the Ohio-Michigan War). The Toledo War was a boundary dispute. Michigan and Ohio formed militias in an attempt to establish state boundaries that would have included a 468 square mile strip of land, now known as the "Toledo Strip".

In December 1836, the Michigan territorial government surrendered the land in exchange for its statehood and approximately three-quarters of the Upper Peninsula. Despite losing the "war", the exchange turned out well for Michigan, when they later discovered copper and the abundant lumber in the Upper Peninsula.

When the state boundaries were established, there was

about 200 acres of land at the tip of the Lost Peninsula, in Ohio, that was north of the Ohio state line. This small section of land became part of Erie, Michigan.

Residents have Michigan addresses and are required to have Michigan License plates and drivers licenses. The state of Ohio does not allow the trucks of Michigan electric companies to drive through the peninsula. Therefore, whenever Consumers Power goes out to work on an electrical problem in this area, the truck first has to be towed to the location. For certain building projects, residents are required to get permits from both states. Ohio residents that work at businesses on the Lost Peninsula have to pay Michigan taxes, even if they drive less than a block to work from Ohio.

There is a stone monument at the Lost Peninsula Marina that commemorates the Toledo War. The monument marks the spot where the Michigan and Ohio governors met to decide where the state line was going to be. What resulted was this unique section of land isolated apart from its state.

Michigan's Continental Divide

There are four or five major continental divides in North America. However, are you aware that there is a mini continental divide in Michigan's Upper Peninsula? A continental divide is a specific point in the land where water splits from its source and travels in different directions.

In the high country of the Porcupine Mountains in Michigan's Upper Peninsula are several unique springs. If you were to stand, straddling over one of the springs, with one foot on the left side and the other on the right side you would see two rivers in their infancy. The water bubbling up from the spring flows in one direction, heading south, eventually forming a river that runs to Lake Michigan. From the same spring, water also flows to the north, shaping a river that continues to Lake Superior.

This unique location is demonstrating an interesting balancing point of nature. The land mass pinnacle is the mid-point between Michigan's two inland seas; lakes Michigan and Superior. You can stand on this precise point and experience two subtle forces of nature. The calm, quiet ripples from the simple spring are the zenith of two titanic forces, manifesting tremendous power. There are not very many places in the world where this happens.

The Mystic Rainbow

In a secret place, when the time is right… it appears. It only happens at certain times, when the inter-play of sunlight and shadow come together at their ordained angles. The rays of light shine through the corridors of the forest, and shine upon the mist produced by a majestic waterfall. Suddenly, there it is, the "Mystic Rainbow." It is as if the rainbow will only appear when all the mechanisms of an ancient woodland time-keeping device are all in their proper places. The rainbow harmoniously appears like the "chimes" of a natural outdoor clock.

At this location on the Black River, in the Upper Peninsula, the ground just opens up and swallows the river. The river vanishes as it drops over a eighty foot waterfall. As the river cascades over this waterfall, it throws up a mist. Suddenly, there is a rainbow stretching from the bottom of the water up to the top. It only happens at certain times. There cannot be any wind and the sun has to shine on it just right. "This is a very unique and hidden place", says Greg Wright. "We do not even know if there is a name for this waterfall. We just call it Rainbow Falls. Every time you go there, it's different. From morning to noon, it changes."

"When we go there, there is never anybody there. You can catch Brown Trout, or at least get bites just about every time you throw in a line," says Wright.

Isn't that strange? You would think this is a good place to catch "*Rainbow*" Trout. This odd spectacle is located on the west side of the Porcupine Mountains, near the town of Besemer.

From the top of Rainbow Falls

The River that Flows Both Ways

Greg Wright, owner of the Thundering Aspen Hunting Lodge near Mesick knows of an incredible phenomenon in the Upper Peninsula.

Somewhere in the wilds of the western Upper Peninsula is the river that flows both ways, with class 4 rapids. The water for the river comes down from the high country. Over about a mile stretch, the water for the river drops in elevation around 1000 to 1500 feet. As you walk down this river, you can see that it is picking up speed.

As the water reaches this lower area, and is picking up tremendous speed, there is a place where the river has cut a very narrow gorge into the rock. At the end of this narrow gorge is a hole. The rushing water, going into this narrow gorge has picked up tremendous speed and pressure by the time it has reached this hole.

The water shoots straight out of the hole from this gorge at cannon strength. The water blasts into a rock across from the hole. It hits the rock and splits the river in half. One-half of the river continues down the gorge. The other half of the river smashes into the rock with such velocity, that it somehow bounces off and begins flowing in the opposite direction up hill for a while. Then it bends back and flows back down hill. This site is described as being unbelievable.

Directions as to how to get to this spot are just about impossible to explain. Hunting guide Greg Wright may be one of the few people that can take you there. At this spectacular place, you can watch one river flowing in two directions at once.

If you have an unusual
fact or phenomenon
about the great state of Michigan
or about an odd Michigander
and would like to see your story
in a future edition of
"*MYSTIC MICHIGAN*",
please send your information to:

Zosma Publications
P.O. Box 24
Hersey, Michigan 49639
zosmabooks@gmail.com

Explore the Phenomenal in Michigan's Nature –
Discover the Bizarre in Michigan's Past with the
MYSTIC MICHIGAN SERIES

MYSTIC MICHIGAN PART 1-
Pictured Rocks – Floating Island –Largest Living Creature – Sanilac Petroglyphs – The Cadillac to Traverse City Indian Trail – The Legend of Lake Superior – Missaukee Mounds – Underwater Passages – The Ancient Forest – Michigan Pyramids – Michigan's Mystery Culture –Sea Monster – Bigfoot in Michigan – Treasure Troves – Mystery Canal – Michigan Mirage – Sinkholes – Michigan's Place on the Continent of Pangaea – Gravity Hill – Paulding Lights – Waterfalls – Caves – Ancient Volcanoes – Great Lakes Triangle – Strange Prehistoric Creatures – Meteorites – Michigan's Stonehenge – Ancient Michigan Tablets – Dolmen Altars – St. Elmo's Fire – Ghost Fire – Waterspouts – Green Sunsets – Raining Fish – Tornados of Fire – Water Running UP Hill – Ancient Geometrical Gardens – Spirit Island – Strange Shakings in Michigan – Michigan Dust Devils – Michigan Man Eaters – Sinking City – Ancient Statues – Weird Weather Patterns – Vikings in Michigan – The Village of Giants – Bottomless Lakes – The Island of Ill Repute – Ice Storms

MYSTIC MICHGAN PART 2-
Ancient Underwater Indian Trail – Mysterious Ancient Wall – Ancient Rivers of Fire – Michigan's Life Energy Scientist – Kitch-iti-kipi Michigan's Emerald Spring – Vanishing Stream – Mystery Stones – Floating Bridge – Bizarre Bird Attacks – Disappearing and reappearing Lake – Glowing Graves – Dinosaurs in Michigan – Living Headless Animal – Tallest People – Bizarre Deer encounters – Illusions of Gravity – Artesian Will City – Fantastic Ice Caves – Bridge of Stars – Hobos in Michigan – An Unusual Michigander – Above Ground Cemeteries – Ancient Circular Ruins – Invisible Mountain – Fireballs From the Skies – Ball Lightning – Disappearing Land Masses

MYSTIC MICHIGAN PART 3-
Gogamain, Michigan's Kingdom of Darkness – Strange Underwater Fish Sounds – Magical Singing Mouse – Passenger Pigeon – Earthquakes in Michigan – Michigan's Highest Point – Winter Wonderland Snow Secrets – Secret Weather Omens – Subconscious Designs – Strange Glowing Fungus – Cosmic Radio Station – Angel Encounter – Buried City - Faces in the Falls – Incredible Echo Chambers – Tree Tunnels – Invisible Walls – Ghost Towns – The Lake Michigan Blob- Nature Drums – Primitive Rock Paintings- Age Old Disc Factory – Ancient Observations – Mystic Earth Rings – Mysterious Missing Race – Enchanted Forest – Healing Forests – Mazes – Hypnotic Animals – Water Riddles

MYSTIC MICHIGAN PART 4-
Ruins of Rome – Mystic Tower – Mermaid – Michigan: Ancient Cemetery – 1999 Fireball Phenomenon – Subterranean World – Hemlock Lights – Treasure Island Hermit – Strange Animal Encounters – Lake Erie's Fairy Grotto – Underwater Forest – Michigan's Circle and Square – Lights of Denton Road – Reappearing Historic Ship – Forest Cemeteries – Lost Gold Mine – Underwater Metropolis – Medieval Michigan – Explosion Oddity – Strange Earth Design – Strange Rivers – Underwater Roads – Will-o-wisp – House of David – Rock Face – Island Treasure – Geometric Formations – Ancient Underwater Structure – Meteorite Islands

MYSTIC MICHIGAN PART 5-
Walled Lake – Phantom Train – Oakwood Cemetery Gravity Hill – Phantom Ships – Norway Forest Light – Mystic Stream – The Portage Lake Story – Buried Prehistoric Beast – Bellevue Ruins – Balloon Bombs in Michigan – Haserot Beach Mystery – Unusual Boulder – Huge Ancient Cataclysm – Mysterious Garden Island – Stannard Rock – Strange Grand Rapids Mound – Ancient 1,000 Acre Garden – Disappearing House – Strange Lake Craters – Ancient Stairway – Michigan's Biggest Trees – Mystery Sphere – Labyrinth – Ancient 2 Acre Horseshoe – Underwater Casino – Acid Lake – Shoe Tree – An Amazing Canyon – Michigan's Scandinavian Landscape

MYSTIC MICHIGAN PART 6-
Crop Circles - More Michigan Mastodons - Whispering Waters – Whirlpools - Stationary Whirlwind - Great Lake Sharks - Flying Campfires - Ancient Parking Lots - Iargo Springs - Strange Animal Screams - Underground Factory - Ancient Cemetery Island - Mystic Lights of Paris - Durant's Castle - Meteorite Fires - Hexen Rings - Singing Sands - Michigan's Giant Gem - Underwater Sinkholes - Underwater Mountains - Ancient Buried Forest - Great Lakes Catastrophe - Ancient Underwater Woodland - Natural underwater Monument - Underwater Maze - Michigan's Earthwork Alignments - Michigan Mimetoliths - Ancient River Beds

MYSTIC MICHIGAN PART 7-
Ancient War Mine - The Bottle House - Stone Chambers - Pre- Glacial - Turnip Rock - Eerie Pere Cheney - The Legend of Silver Mountain - Magnetic Abnormality - The Michigan/Wizard of Oz Connection - Ancient Explosion - King Solomon's Mines? - Michigan's Brigadoon - Huge Statues - Echo Canyons - Wilderness Column of Water - Michigan's New Stonehenge - Amazing Dunes - Arrowhead Finds - The Orbs of Nunica Cemetery - Ancient Library of Rock - A Very Large Piece of Copper - Phenomenal Painting - Michigan's Lost Peninsula - Michigan's Continental Divide - The Mystic Rainbow - The River That Flows Both Ways

MYSTIC MICHGANDER
MYSTIC MICHIGAN PART 1 AUDIOBOOK
TRIPPING AMERICA THE FANTASTIC

ORDER FORM

The following items are available by
Mark Jager

Qty.	Item	Total
_____	Mystic Michigan #1... $8.95	_____ .
_____	Mystic Michigan #2... $8.95	_____ .
_____	Mystic Michigan #3... $8.95	_____ .
_____	Mystic Michigan #4... $8.95	_____ .
_____	Mystic Michigan #5... $8.95	_____ .
_____	Mystic Michigan #6... $8.95	_____ .
_____	Mystic Michigan #7... $8.95	_____ .
_____	Mystic Michigander... $8.95	_____ .
_____	Mystic Michigan #1 Audio Book ... $12.95	_____ .
_____	Tripping America The Fantastic ... $8.95	_____ .
	SUBTOTAL	_____ .
	SHIPPING	_____ .
	SALES TAX 6%	_____ .
	TOTAL	_____ .

SHIPPING CHARGES

Please send $3.50 for shipping & handling for the first item purchased. Add .25¢ for each additional item.

THANK YOU!

Name_____

Street_____

City_____State_____Zip_____

Send order with check or money order to:

Zosma Publications
PO Box 24
Hersey, MI 49639

Orders ship USPS
Allow 1 week for delivery

Made in the USA
Middletown, DE
23 June 2015